Scottish Class

Volume Three - The 1990s

In railway terms, the decade of the 1990s will never be remembered as classic. Many of the original classes of diesel and electric locomotives built in the 1960s were withdrawn and scrapped and train journeys that were once considered important and prestigious, with first class compartments and buffet carriages, were swept away by a tide of plastic, unsuitable and inapt multiple units. So much history was lost too, what with mail and parcels previously carried in the brake van being transferred to road. The 1990s were also a period of significant change behind the scenes with the full privatisation of Britain's railways being completed.

For enthusiasts and in particular followers of the Class 37 in Scotland, the decade started well but ended fairly bleakly, with mass withdrawals and the familiar Type 3 hauled train being powered by the ubiquitous Class 66. It wasn't all doom and gloom as there were some significant 'Tractor' highlights in the 1990s. The pairs of 37s on sleeper services to Aberdeen and Inverness was just one, but the inability of the modern units to cope with the peaks and troughs of Scottish tourism led to some sensational and unforgetable passenger train workings by some of the rarest Class 37s in the history of railways! "It's massive mate" as they said and sure enough, it was!

This volume covers Scottish Class 37s throughout the 1990s. Once again I've cheated ever so slightly with a few images from 1989 but I think it is important to show how the 1980s ended and the new decade began. In addition, apologies now for the position of the photo captions. With so many railway magazines and books publishing postage-stamp size images I have an incredible enthusiasm for full page pictures, in particular of landscape shots, so the captions - as per Volume Two - are not always where you expect them, but they are there - honest!

My sincere thanks go to John Hooson and Andrew Donnelly for allowing me to use what I consider to be some of the best images ever taken of Class 37s in Scotland. I am truly honoured to use them and to John in particular, thank you for climbing those mountains and chasing the sunshine. I now understand why the months of March and April are better than June and July! Further thanks are extended to John and Andrew for their help in researching the captions; to Peter Scott for his images and 'moves'; to Jim Ramsay for his slides and superb knowledge of Scottish railways; to John Griffiths and finally David Umpleby, Mary, Elizabeth and Jason for their extensive help and understanding, which makes all this possible.

Enjoy the book
Nick Meskell
February 2007

ISBN 0-9548035-8-2   First Published 2007
All rights reserved. No part of this book may be reproduced or transmitted in any form or by any means, electronic or mechanical, including photocopying, scanning, recording or by any information storage and retrieval system, without permission from the Publisher in writing. **Printed by Goodman Bayliss, Worcester**

Future Releases:

I originally planned to produce a series of three books on Scottish 37s, the first covering the Steam Heat years 1980-1984, the second the 37/4 years from 1985 to 1989 and this third book was supposed to cover 1990 to the present day. However, as is often the case, new images - previously unpublished - and new information has come forward. In addition, this series of books has become very popular so further volumes will be produced over the next three or four years. This volume now covers the entire 1990s. Volume four will cover 2000 onwards, bringing the Scottish Class 37 story right up to date. Volume five will then go back to the very start, with the 1980s revisited, covering the Steam Heat years and the early days of 37s in more detail. Release dates have not yet been decided for these books. There are also other Scottish subjects in the pipeline. The previously advertised cover for Volume Three, will now form the basis of Volume Four as seen below:

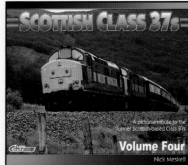

This title will be released in 2008

LOCOMOTIVE POOLS AND BOOKED PASSENGER TRAINS

Although this is a pictorial book, it's important to get an idea of which locomotives were based in Scotland in the 1990s and which trains they were booked to haul. Unfortunately it is not possible to list every train and every locomotive. Instead, a snapshot of the 1992-1994 period is provided which, according to aficionados of the Scottish Class 37, may well have been the best years of the decade. By this time, locomotives were split into operating pools and following the closure of Eastfield, there were three pools at Inverness and three at Motherwell which pretty much encompassed all passenger and freight work north of the border. For Inverness, it was the RAJV, RAJP and IISA pools which, during the period covered, housed a credible 46 machines. RAJV signified Regional Railways Infrastructure Scotrail Inverness Class 37, while RAJP was the same except it housed 37/4s. The IISA pool was the Inter City sponsored pool of 37/0s and 37/5s for the overnight sleeper services between Edinburgh, Aberdeen and Inverness plus any Inter City Landcruises or luxury trains. At Motherwell, locos in the MDRM pool worked Railfreight Distribution trains while FCPM was for Trainload Coal and Petroleum. A small pool of 37/7s worked in the LGPM pool. Looking back, all this sectorisation was a load of mumbo jumbo as so called Coal and Petroleum 37/4 machines ended up on the Fort William sleeper and Inverness Infrastructure locos hauled luxury landcruises, plus it was difficult to keep track of the never ending changes! Loco liveries from this period can be seen throughout the book but there was definitely an overkill of Civil Engineers 'Dutch' and various shades of grey with or without branding. The table below records which locos represented which pools from this time but it should be noted that they were not all in the pool at the same time. For example, 37402 and 37404 were only working for RAJV for a short period, while the high numbered 37/5s in the IISA pool were latecomers:

Inverness RAJV pool

37004	37025	37043	37048
37051	37069	37087	37088
37099	37106	37153	37156
37165	37167	37184	37196
37201	37212	37232	37240
37255	37275	37294	37351
37402	37404		

Mon to Fri - Summer 1993
Loco 1
1T16 09.45 Inverness - Glasgow QS
1H03 13.33 Glasgow QS - Inverness

Loco 2
2H80 07.00 Kyle - Inverness
2H85 12.35 Inverness - Kyle
2H86 17.05 Kyle - Inverness

Loco 3
2H83 10.25 Inverness - Kyle
2H84 15.10 Kyle - Inverness
2H87 18.38 Inverness - Kyle

Inverness RAJP pool

37427	37428	37431

Mon to Fri - Summer 1993
Loco 1
1B26 10.15 Inverness - Edinburgh
1H15 15.35 Edinburgh - Inverness

Loco 2
1A44 05.52 Inverness - Aberdeen
1H27 09.20 Aberdeen - Inverness
1A52 12.20 Inverness - Aberdeen
1H33 15.16 Aberdeen - Inverness

Loco 3
2P10 07.08 Perth - Edinburgh
1H11 11.25 Edinburgh - Inverness
1B36 16.28 Inverness - Edinburgh
2P47 21.18 Edinburgh - Perth

Inverness IISA pool

37080	37113	37133	37152
37170	37175	37194	37214
37221	37250	37251	37262
37285	37505	37510	37683
37685			

Mon to Fri - Summer 1993
Locos 1+2 (2 x 37)
1S25 04.10 Edinburgh - Inverness
(20.55 Euston - Inverness)
1M16 20.20 Inverness - Edinburgh
(continued to London Euston)

Locos 3+4 (2 x 37)
1S79 04.45 Edinburgh - Aberdeen
(22.03 Euston - Aberdeen
1M12 21.25 Aberdeen - Edinburgh
(continued to London Euston)

Motherwell FCPM pool (No booked passenger work)

37051	37066	37071	37100	37111	37184	37188	37212
37262	37403	37404	37409	37690	37692	37693	37695
37696	37714						

Motherwell MDRM pool

37401	37406	37410	37423
37424	37430		

Mon to Fri - Summer 1993
Loco 1
1Y11 03.30 Edinburgh - Fort William
(21.05 Euston - Fort William)
1Y12 08.55 F. William - Glasgow QS
1Y13 14.20 Glasgow QS - F. William
1B01 19.50 Fort William - Edinburgh
(continued to London Euston)

Note: 1Y12 and 1Y13 only ran on certain dates. The northbound sleeper was 1S07 returning south as 1M15. Unlike today, all three sleeper services ran as separate trains to/from London Euston.

Motherwell LGPM pool
(No booked passenger work)

37712	37801	37893

Opposite: We start our review of passenger services in 1989 with 37406 'The Saltire Society' working 1H09, the 09.33 Glasgow Queen Street to Inverness on 25th August. The train pauses at the picturesque station of Kingussie, 46.5 miles south of Inverness, which was about 45 minutes from journey's end. The 37/4 was substituting for an unavailable 47, but was spot on time, so it was not an en-route failure. Providing the loco stuck to diagram, it was booked south with 1B34, the 14.45 to Edinburgh and then 1H01, the overnight 23.25 Edinburgh to Inverness. From conversion in 1985, this loco was in Large Logo livery until a repaint in what was known at the time as Mainline (or Inter City Mainline) and at this time in 1989, 37406 was working in Eastfield's FGXX pool which hosted locos for Speedlink Distribution trains. Today, 37406 is a real survivor and, painted in EWS livery and still named, the loco is a regular on the Powderhall to Oxwellmains 'binliner' train. *(John Hooson)*

Above: Class 37s were never associated with the push-pull trains of the 1980s but on 28th September 1989, 37066 was used to help out following a series of failures. Passengers on the 07.25 Glasgow Queen Street to Aberdeen service had an extended and interesting journey after firstly, 47712 failed prior to departure with a push-pull fault, hence 47541 was used instead. This loco only made it to Stirling before it too gave up! Next, 37066 was stolen from a northbound Speedlink service to remove the errant 47 before coupling up and carrying on alone as far as Dundee, complete with a full Scotrail liveried push pull set in tow! Having provided the photographer with a most amusing morning, 37066 ran round its stock and returned ECS to Cowlairs, seen here powering away out of Dundee station. This former north east stalwart was still displaying its trademark Thornaby embellishments despite being a Tinsley loco at the time! It later spent two years at Motherwell in 1993/1994. *(Andrew Donnelly)*

Opposite: A truly stunning image of an equally remarkable combination at Drumochter summit on 27th April 1989. As the story goes, the previous day's 12.00 Kings Cross to Inverness had been Class 37 hauled north through Dalwhinnie late that evening due to an unknown fault. Stabling overnight at Inverness, it was not possible to repair the defect so another 37 was turned out for the following days 08.00 Inverness to Kings Cross. Inverness stalwart 37261 'Caithness' did the honours and with two dead power cars and eight Mk3s in tow, the train was doing pretty well, only about 20 minutes down at this stage. The introduction of 'Sprinter' DMUs on the Far North lines in January 1989 had ended the Class 37 monopoly on passenger services. A number of 37s were still based at Inverness for freight duties such as 37070, 37109 and 37175 plus the old trio of 37260 'Radio Highland', 37261 'Caithness' and 37262 'Dounreay' although by this time all three had had their steam heat boilers isolated. *(John Hooson)*

Opposite: Trainload Metals on the Highland Main Line at Dalnaspidal with 37423 'Sir Murray Morrison' on 22nd May 1989 working 1H13, the 13.33 Glasgow Queen Street to Inverness. This was another Class 47 substitution and the diagram started at Inverness and finished at Edinburgh. The train is formed: TSO+BSO+TSO+TSOT+BFK which offered 214 standard class seats, 24 first class seats (in four compartments), a micro buffet counter service and plenty of room for luggage, bicycles, mail and parcels in two half brakes. *(John Hooson)*

Above: On 16th July 1990, 37240 replaced a failed Class 47 at Perth on the previous night's 21.00 Euston to Inverness sleepers. Running three hours late, the train finally rolled into Kingussie station, the loco having been reduced to almost walking pace on the final stages of the climb up Drumochter summit despite the outrageous thrash! Whilst waiting for a southbound service to pass, 37240 could at least recover a bit of composure prior to the assault on Slochd. This loco arrived in Scotland in January of the same year, becoming part of Eastfield's DCHA pool and then a member of the RAJV pool at Inverness, prior to moving to Bescot in May 1995. *(Andrew Donnelly)*

Page 10: Anybody unfamiliar with Scottish railway history may well believe that the Class 47 locomotive was notoriously unreliable and often failed. This may be partially correct, (in the early 1990s anyway) judging by the number of Class 37 substitutions featured so far but they did work successfully for decades, prior to their 1990s downfall. Drumochter summit again, this time on 4th May 1990 with a very clean 37087 atop 'The Clansman', 1S59, the 07.35 London Euston to Inverness. The train was over 80 minutes late at this point following the failure of the 47 further south which was duly removed allowing Type 3 power to take over. Without an ETH supply it may have been a little stuffy in the carriages but with an English Electric monster on the front, it was a noisy ride north. With sealed connecting doors on 37087, this former Eastern Region machine opened its Scottish account with a move from Tinsley to Eastfield in March 1990 and then up to Inverness in February 1992. Today, this loco is working for DRS, based at Carlisle. *(John Hooson)*

Page 11: Heavyweight action in the Highlands with Trainload Petroleum branded 37707 (formerly 37001) near Dalwhinnie also on 4th May 1990 (clearly a bad day for Scottish 47s). 47461 'Charles Rennie Mackintosh' had departed from Inverness with 1T30, the 12.30 Inverness to Glasgow Queen Street but failed north of Dalwhinnie. Following behind was 37707 with a rake of 18 wagons which pushed the 47 and its train to Dalwhinnie station itself. Here the wagons were uncoupled, 37707 ran round and topped the 47 through to Glasgow. Amazingly, 37707 returned north with 1H03, the 18.03 to Inverness before a return to Dalwhinnie light engine to collect its wagons and head south. *(John Hooson)*

Opposite: In summer 1993 loco-hauled turns over the Highland Main Line were somewhat dominated by the Inverness based Class 37/4s with the likes of ex-Eastfield machines 37402 and 37404 powering many services. The following year saw considerably more unrefurbished Class 37/0s being used and these included many examples previously dedicated to freight pools which, in turn, hadn't worked passenger trains for years. On a glorious 2nd September 1993, 37175 was entrusted with the Highland Enterprise turn, 1B26 the 10.15 Inverness to Edinburgh and 1H15, the 15.40 return. The latter is seen here hammering away from the capital at South Gyle. Despite an overhaul into Civil Engineers 'Dutch' livery, the former West Highland stalwart retains the mounting for the spotlight-style headlight above the headcode boxes. *(Andrew Donnelly)*

Above: One of the well known Eastfield Class 37s was 37043, the former 'Loch Lomond'. Having been displaced from the West Highlands by the class 37/4s, the loco was reallocated to Stratford, working in the Trainload Construction pool and via an overhaul at Crewe works in 1988, was renumbered as 37354, having been fitted with re-geared CP7 bogies. Four years later, it returned to Inverness as 37043 when standard bogies were refitted along with a repaint into 'Dutch'. As part of the RAJV pool it made regular appearances on the summer only hauled turns including a regular spell on the Highland Enterprise turn in September 1993. With an increased load of seven Mk2s, 37043 pounds up the gradient towards Plean on the climb out of the Forth Valley from Stirling with the 10.15 from Inverness on 2nd September 1993. 37043 remained in Scotland at Motherwell, prior to being stored in June 1999. It languished at Wigan CRDC for parts removal until 2002 after which it was purchased by DRS hopefully for a return to service. In the end it was stripped prior to eventual disposal in 2003. *(Andrew Donnelly)*

Page 14: 37402 'Oor Wullie' pictured south of Wade's Bridge, Dalwhinnie on 26th May 1993 with 1B36, the 16.28 Inverness to Edinburgh. Although starting out its life as a 37/4 based at Eastfield, this loco probably gained more fame in later years in South Wales for its role on the Cardiff - Rhymney circuit. Of the thirty-one Class 37/4s converted, 17 examples were painted in this Inter City colour scheme. *(John Hooson)*

Page 15: Following the withdrawal of Inter City support and the reallocation of the 47/6s (47/4s with long range fuel tanks), a local initiative saw the introduction of Class 37/4s and the repainting of several sets of coaching stock into this striking new livery, latterly known as 'Regional Railways'. 37427 (formerly 'Bont Y Bermo') was transferred from Cardiff and repainted to match. In a ceremony at Inverness on 17th May 1993, the loco was named 'Highland Enterprise' for the newly created Inverness - Edinburgh services. As it turned out, 37427 was a one-off thus making this image of matching locomotive and carriages unique. The photo is at Ralia, just seven days after the naming ceremony and the train is the correct one, 1B26, the 10.15 Inverness to Edinburgh. *(John Hooson)*

Opposite: For two weeks in July 1993, the Forth Bridge was closed for engineering work resulting in Edinburgh - Inverness workings being diverted via Stirling. This included the 11.25 loco-hauled turn which on 9th July featured 37431, captured thundering north at Bardrill Road. Distinctively, the former Cardiff machine 'Bullidae' retained its unique Trainload Petroleum logos on the secondman's cabsides. The loco was not the most reliable performer during 1993 and was more commonly found on the Kyle and Aberdeen turns or stabled at Inverness with electrical troubles. *(Andrew Donnelly)*

Above: Despite never having been associated with Scotland, 37113 gained the name 'Radio Highland' from 37260, after the latter was withdrawn in 1989 following fire damage. 37113 was reprieved from withdrawal itself, overhauled at Doncaster works and placed in the Inverness Speedlink pool as a direct replacement for 37260. Ironically the loco did not have the RETB equipment with which its name was associated! In 1991 the loco drifted south into the Tinsley Railfreight Distribution pool, prior to returning north to Inverness two years later as part of the Inter City sleeper (IISA) pool. By the following year it was allocated to Regional Railways departmental pool (RAJV) and as such became a regular on the Highland Main Line passenger workings. On 23rd July 1994 it was entrusted with the 14.30 Inverness to Edinburgh, seen heading south away from Dalwhinnie. This very turn became 37113s final working as exactly three weeks later, on 13th August, it ran away from Waverley station after the parking brake leaked off whilst waiting to run round its stock. The loco collided head-on with HST Power car 43180 at Abbeyhill, causing severe damage to both, although thankfully without serious injury to staff or passengers. As a result, the second 'Radio Highland' was cut for scrap at Portobello the following August by MC Metals. *(Andrew Donnelly)*

Above: During the strike afflicted summer season of 1994, Scotrail ran additional loco-hauled services from Glasgow Queen Street Low Level to Oban and Fort William on varying days of the week. The Oban services seemed to coincide with the signalling staff strike action more than the Fort William turns and did not run on too many occasions. However, 27th August saw 37170 returning to its former stamping ground with the 09.50 from Glasgow, which then formed the 16.00 return as seen here having run round at Oban. During the shunting and watering of the stock, staff were insistent that everyone had to leave the platforms because of safety issues. Obviously several years of Sprinter-only operation had changed the previously casual approach and was one of the very rare occasions of an example of unfriendly staff in the Highlands. *(Andrew Donnelly)*

Opposite: The first of a series of images of the Inverness - Kyle of Lochalsh line and by 1990, only two Large Logo liveried Class 37/4s survived at Inverness, namely 37418 and 37421. The latter is seen here on the lightly loaded 15.30 Kyle of Lochalsh to Inverness, seen departing from Muir of Ord on 25th July. Coincidentally this working passed 37418 heading west with the 17.55 to Kyle. This pair left Scotland together, joining the Petroleum sector at Immingham and subsequently the North Wales Coast pool based at Crewe and they became 'East Lancashire Railway' and 'The Kingsman' with repaints into the Regional Railways livery. After returning to Motherwell, both were withdrawn from service in April 2005. *(Andrew Donnelly)*

Below: Having spent the morning of 17th July 1990 on ballast duty, 37156 was turned out by Inverness for the 12.27 to Kyle and with less than 100 tons in tow, this four vehicle affair is seen trundling west towards Beauly. This loco spent by far the great majority of its career in Scotland, having moved north from Landore in 1966, it spent the next 24 years at Polmadie and Motherwell on arduous freight work around the west of Scotland, including a spell renumbered as 37311. By 1990, it had become part of the Civil Engineers pool at Eastfield and was later to spend time at Inverness in the sleeper pool, prior to its first allocation to England as part of Bescot's Transrail fleet in 1995. The loco was named 'British Steel Hunterston' at Motherwell in March 1986 when it became 37311. This name was retained upon renumbering back to 37156 and a coat of all over grey. *(Andrew Donnelly)*

Opposite: During 1990 one diagram which was frequently used by Inverness as a 'kick out' turn was the 09.00 to Elgin and 10.18 return. No heat 37/0s often featured prior to them taking up their booked Speedlink working over the Highland Main Line in the afternoon. The misty morning of 25th July 1990 had cleared by the time former Far North star 37262 'Dounreay' appeared at Miltonduff with the 10.18 from Elgin. Despite having been transferred to Eastfield's Speedlink pool some two months earlier after eight years at Inverness, 37262 was still a regular sight in the area on freight workings. After a brief spell at Tinsley, 'Dounreay' returned home in September 1992 for a further three years as part of the Inter City sleeper and later departmental pools. *(Andrew Donnelly)*

'DUTCH' TO KYLE

Anybody following the Inverness Class 37 scene in the 1980s may have become bored with the same seven locos. New day, new year, new timetable and still it was 37017, 37025, 37035, 37114, 37260, 37261 and 37262 with their steam heat boilers and latterly, headlights and radios. These seven machines really represented the Far North scene from plain BR Blue to Large Logo years. In their place came a whole new selection of 37s, aimed specifically at freight services but occasionally used on passenger trains. With Wick and Thurso services in the hands of Class 156 DMUs, the 37 at Georgemas Junction had long gone but the growl of Tractor power could still be found on the Kyle line. Regular visitors in 1993 were: 37025, 37043, 37087, 37099, 37156, 37232 and 37294. These four images show the new era of 'Dutch' locos, Regional Railways and LNER tourist green coaches and a former Class 101 DMU trailer, converted into an observation saloon.... this was certainly the 1990s!

Opposite top: 37196 pictured north east of the avalanche shelter at Cuddies Point, near Attadale, in summer 1993.

Opposite lower: Former Inverness favourite 37025 heads out of Strathcarron with a lengthy seven coach train for Kyle in July 1993. It would appear the first two coaches have been added to increase capacity thus spoiling a perfect green and cream formation. Observation Saloon 6300 is in its correct place on the rear, offering passengers unimpededed views for a fare supplement. This coach was formerly numbered 54356, a Class 101 driver trailer built in 1958, and converted for this special role in 1987, with a seating capacity of 42.

Top: An unidentified Class 37 passes the classic location at Craig Highland Farm with 12.28 Inverness to Kyle.

Opposite: Two loco hauled trains at Kyle. Here on 6th July 37232 'The Institution of Railway Signal Engineers' stands in the usual departure platform while another 37 and rake of stock are stabled adjacent. *(All photos: John Griffiths)*

AFTER DARK

Below: Having been displaced from the cut-off Far North and Kyle lines, the fleet of Inverness based Class 37/4s were regularly used between 1989 and 1991 vice Class 47s on the Highland Main Line. Principal 37 turns were the 07.00 and 12.30 Inverness to Glasgow Queen Street, returning with the 13.33 and 18.03 respectively. Locos marooned north of the Ness bridge collapse were exchanged as they became due exams, with a pair normally to be found south of the breach. On the bitterly cold evening of 2nd February 1990, 37416 was to be found heading home with the 18.03 ex-Queen Street, seen here under the lights of Perth station during a crew change.
(Andrew Donnelly)

Opposite: The more demanding of the Highland Main Line turns in 1993 involved the 07.08 Perth to Edinburgh via Stirling, thence 11.25 to Inverness and 16.28 return routed via Fife, before returning to Perth with the 21.22, again via Stirling. During the summer season, dedicated 37427 'Highland Enterprise' was more normally employed on its' namesake train, the 10.15 Inverness to Edinburgh and 15.35 return, so its appearance on the Perth turn on 10th September was notable. The train is seen prior to departure from Waverley's rainswept platform 21.
(Andrew Donnelly)

Page 27: The night of 26th September 1992 should have seen the last working of the small Inverness pool of class 47/6s (47671-47677) on Highland Main Line workings, the final turn being the 16.28 Inverness to Edinburgh thence 21.22 to Perth. However, Inverness turned out Inter City liveried 37152 for these workings, seen during the run round at Waverley. This loco had a very similar history to 37156, having been christened 'British Steel Ravenscraig' between 1986 and 1990 whilst renumbered as 37310 as part of a dedicated fleet supplying its namesake steel plant. The loco became one of three class 37/0s (37221 and 37251 being the others) repainted into Inter City Swallow livery for working the Inverness and Aberdeen sleepers north of Edinburgh from May 1992. Displaced from these turns in 1995, it remained in Scotland on freight work based at Motherwell until being stored at Bescot depot in late 1999. After several years in open store, it was purchased for preservation in 2005, moving to Peak Rail the following year. *(Andrew Donnelly)*

All is quiet at Perth depot on 26th August 1993 with 37428 'David Lloyd George' and a rake of coaches as they wait to work the 07.08 to Edinburgh the following morning. Transferred from Cardiff to Grangemouth in January 1991, this loco was repainted with Trainload Petroleum branding following overhaul and became the only ever 37/4 in this livery to work in Scotland. *(Nick Meskell collection)*

Page 28: In 1992 seven Class 47s, numbered 47671-47677, were working the Highland Main Line. All were named and liveries included Large Logo and Inter City Executive. They were far from reliable and the introduction of pairs of Class 37s on Sleeper services must have been a relief for British Rail and the long suffering passengers. Although photogenic, the problems of a serious train failure on a single line railway can be catastrophic for all other freight and passenger services for the remainder of the day! Running a staggering 155 minutes late, 37209 hauls 47674 north past Ralia on 20th May 1992. The 37 had come from Inverness to rescue the train. *(John Hooson)*

Page 29: Power to the people or at least to those on 1S25, the 21.30 London Euston to Inverness on 26th May 1993. Reminiscent of when pilot locos were attached at Perth or Blair Atholl in days of steam, 37170 leads the way with 37251 tucked inside. Due to their low Electric Train Supply (ETS) index, pairs of Class 37/4s were of no use on this service. ETS for the entire train was provided by a generator coach behind the locos so whether 37/0, 37/4 or 37/5, the train was warm and air conditioned. *(John Hooson)*

SLEEPER TRAINS

Centre pages: Thunder in the mountains at Drumochter summit on 19th May 1994 with 37510 and 37069 as they hammer up the 18 mile climb from Blair Atholl. Surrounded by 3000+ feet mountain tops, the 37s breast the 1484 feet summit after the laborious climb - much of it 1 in 70. The photographer and many others considered this (1S25) to be the train of the year in 1994 and the approaching growl on this particular day could be heard for a full 15 minutes! The 12 coaches in tow include the generator coach behind the locos and two Motorail vehicles (GUV) on the rear. In the summer an extra two GUVs were added. Remarkably both 37069 and 37510 avoided the scrapman and are alive and well in 2007, working for DRS - although you won't find them on the Highland Main Line! *(John Hooson)*

Below: With the Inverness and Aberdeen sleepers swapping to Class 47/7 haulage from May 1995, the London Euston to Fort William sleeper duly became the last passenger/sleeper train in Scotland to be booked for a Type 3 and this continued right though until June 2006. Although the West Highland line was very much deprived of 37 hauled passenger trains in the 1990s, as the sole survivor, the photographers returned and 1Y11 and 1B01 became 'the trains' to record. 25th March 1996 with 37409 'Loch Awe' in big 'T' livery with just four miles of its journey to go, drifts through Torlundy. *(John Hooson)*

Opposite: The classic shot of the northbound West Highland sleepers just after leaving Bridge of Orchy station on 15th May 1996. Following overhaul in late 1993, 37403 emerged in this pseudo-BR green livery, acquiring the name 'Ben Cruachan' (from 37404) at the same time. On 1st January 1996 the original thirty one Class 37/4s had been split far and wide with 37401, 37403, 37404, 37406, 37409, 37410, 37423, 37424, 37428, 37430 and 37431 working in Scotland, all based in Motherwell's LGHM pool which was for sleeper, freight and charter trains on the Oban, Fort William and Mallaig lines. *(John Hooson)*

LUXURY TRAINS

Above: The obsession mankind has with mountains, lochs, glens and open landscapes is something on which railways have capitalised since day one and there's no better place than Scotland to enjoy the spendour and grandeur of a million years of circumstance and supervention. From wealthy Japanese and American tourists to Mr. England and his family of four, the train was, is and always will be the unrivaled seat to Scotland's majesty. In the 1990s, the Inter City land cruises conveyed tourists from the south. With Mk3a sleeping stock, first class Mk1 day stock, a kitchen car and a pair of 37s, it was a hotel on wheels and a real financial gain for the smart Inter City marketing bosses of the time. Taken circa-1993, one such land cruise awaits departure south from Inverness with 37170, an Inter City liveried 37 and a Mk1 support/crew coach atop the main train. *(John Griffths)*

Opposite: Probably just about as good as it gets when it comes to railway photography in Scotland in the 1990s. Snow, sunshine, a deep blue loch and a barren landscape culminating in absolute perfection with the passing of 37221+37152 on an overnight land cruise to Kyle of Lochalsh. The date is 14th May 1994 and the location is Achanalt, about 40 miles north of Inverness. The train was recorded as 1H93, the 00.55 from Edinburgh and it followed the Inverness sleeper up the Highland Main Line by about an hour. Considering 1S25 was booked at 04.10 from Edinburgh, 1H93 must have hidden somewhere en-route. Although the train details are given as 00.55 from Edinburgh, the origin would have been somewhere south, probably London and in fact, the 00.55 departure could have been London itself! *(John Hooson)*

Above: Following the demise of all booked freight, passenger and sleeper haulage, the Royal Scotsman is now the last bastion of Class 37 haulage in Scotland although this was threatened during 2006 when Class 33 and 57 locos were used, alongside 37s and 47s. From its conception in 1985, Class 37s provided the power and on 21st May 1989, 37409 'Loch Awe' passes Crubenmore with what was 'The Queen of Scots' set. Behind the loco is 45018, a 1927-built LMS saloon with a DMU end! Next is 5189, a LNWR railway dining car dating to 1891! Third up is a more recently built (!) GNR dining car from 1912, numbered 807! Six Mk1s complete the rake including two sleeping cars. *(John Hooson)*

Opposite: Although the Royal Scotman started out with three regular ex-steam heat locos (37114, 37261 and 37262) by the late 1980s and into the early 1990s, 37/4s were more frequently employed but with many examples transferred to Immingham, Laira or Thornaby for freight duties, 37/0s moved north and took over their work. Pictured near Dalnaspidal on 22nd May 1992, an alien in the form of 37252 powers this luxury train north. Looking pretty horrific in faded Railfreight Distribution branding this is no machine to haul such a prestigious train but it makes a great photo! *(John Hooson)*

Two more examples of alien power on this luxury train and 37214 with Railfreight Construction branding works hard as it passes the site of Elliot Junction near Arbroath on 12th September 1993. By this time the stock was painted in a matching livery and the Mk1 sleeping carriages were still in use. 37214 was based at Inverness in the IISA pool from September 1992 until March 1994 before further moves to Motherwell, Cardiff, Motherwell again, Bescot and then Crewe before final withdrawal in December 1999. In June 2000 the loco arrived at Wigan for scrapping and after more than three years of storage, it was sold and removed to Barrow Hill for restoration. Now under private ownership and sporting a gleaming coat of BR Blue, 37214 was the star attraction at the Keighley and Worth Valley Diesel Gala in June 2005 working 12 round trips between Oxenhope and Keighley including two in multiple with DRS machine 37605. In a similar twist of fate to 37261 (see Volume Two), the loco was then sold to the West Coast Railway Company of Carnforth who had the contract to provide traction for the Royal Scotsman and amazingly, following a repaint in the maroon livery, 37214 was back, hauling this luxury train in the spring and summer of 2006! *(Jim Ramsay/Nick Meskell collection)*

'Dutch' on the Scotsman on 5th September 1993 with 37133 approaching Arbroath. Reallocated to Motherwell in December 1979, this machine was a long standing member of the 37 clan, enjoying stints at Eastfield in the 1980s and Inverness in the 1990s. Other than a couple of months at Cardiff in 1987, 37133 was Scottish based from 1979 to 1995. When first launched back in 1985 it cost £2,200 per person for a week of luxury travel on the Royal Scotsman and this included journeys to Oban, Mallaig, Kyle and Dunrobin Castle plus various stop offs at Keith, Boat of Garten and Edinburgh. By comparison, today there are five regular jaunts from a 'Highland' journey of two nights to the full 'Grand North Western' lasting a full seven nights. Prices... well... for the ultimate luxury in rail travel, they range from £1,680 to £4,980 per person.... and as tasty as that Aberdeen Angus with iced hazelnut parfait with raspberry coulis may be.... you are sadly no longer guaranteed a 37! *(Jim Ramsay/Nick Meskell collection)*

FREIGHT TRAINS

It's back to the Highland Main Line to start our look at freight trains and at Wade's Bridge, Dalwhinnie, 37107 heads north with 7H25, the morning Speedlink service, 03.45 Millerhill to Inverness on 25th August 1989. With a reasonable load in tow, the loco is a typical blue 37 from the period, sporting black headcode boxes and the orange cantrail stripe. Based at Tinsley at this time, 37107 was a Scottish loco for a few months in 1987, before an untimely and gruesome death in 1996 followed by a most tortuous scrapping between 1999 and 2001 which saw the loco body completely removed, leaving just two end cabs and an underframe. *(John Hooson)*

Above: Travelling on the West Highland line in the 1980s, you may well have seen this locomotive on freight. With no boiler and and just vacuum brakes, 37196 was indeed a 'bare bones' machine. In later years it was moved to Laira - just about as far away as possible - and while working off St. Blazey it was the very first Class 37 painted in the stylish Railfreight Red Stripe livery and it was named 'Tre Pol and Pen'. Two years later and amazingly 37196 was back home, shorn of its nameplates and battling the gradients of the Highland Main Line! Waiting out time at Dalwhinnie station on 26th April 1989, 37196 is in charge of 7H25 to Inverness. This was a booked stop not only for the driver to have an unofficial cup of tea with the signalman but also for the passage of the southbound 08.00 Inverness to Kings Cross. *(John Hooson)*

Page 42: An interesting image of the long gone practice of moving Class 08s by rail on the main line. The 08 number was not recorded but the location is the passing loop at Slochd summit on 25th August 1989 and the shunter - with driving rods removed - is returning north to Inverness following an overhaul. 37418 'An Comunn Gaidhealach' provides the power for what is otherwise a short engineers train of mostly empty ballast hoppers. *(John Hooson)*

May Day in 1990 at Drumochter summit with 37154 and the now famous 7H25 Speedlink service with a short rake of tanks. This working came as something of a surprise as the timetable had changed and no morning freight was scheduled north. Millerhill obviously had some wagons which the customer needed urgently so 37154 was summoned and this was the end result. (Note the 'Cockney Sparrow' on the bodyside - the depot emblem of Stratford. What must this sparrow have made of the Eastfield Terrier or the Inverness Stag!). *(John Hooson)*

Page 44: Two images taken four days apart of 6S69, the 16.30 from Dee Marsh Junction to Elgin via Inverness. This is 20th May 1994 with the grey and 'Dutch' combo of 37262 'Dounreay' and 37099 'Clydebridge' heading the empty log train at Drumochter summit. Similar to 7H25 previously, this service often looped the Kings Cross HST at Dalwhinnie. This therefore allowed the photographer two chances at recording this train. Today, 37099 (running as 37324) is preserved at the Gloucestershire and Warwickshire Railway while 37262 was scrapped in February 2004. *(John Hooson)*

Page 45: Four days earlier and 6S69 had an Inter City 37683 at the front with Railfreight Metals branded 37100 inside at Wade's Bridge. This was an interesting period for pairs of 37s on the Highland Main Line. With 6S69 recently retired to run an hour after the sleepers, it was four 37s in 60 minutes, which by anybody's standard was pretty good. With a choice of just about any loco from the IISA or RAJV pools plus Motherwell's FCPM pool, a mixed bag of liveries, names and sub-classes was virtually guaranteed. *(John Hooson)*

Opposite: It wasn't only the Highland Main Line that enjoyed pairs of 37s on freight, the West Highland line also had a regular morning train - 7D19, the 09.51 Corpach Pulp Mill to Mossend. Instead of 37/0s and 37/5s, this service employed 37/4s based at Motherwell. Pictured at Achallader on 22nd March 1996, grey and green machines 37424 and 37403 'Ben Cruachan' head south with a neatly proportioned train of two locos, two china clay wagons, two aluminium ingot wagons and two paper carriers! *(John Hooson)*

Above: 7D19 near Spean Bridge with 37406 'The Saltire Society' and 37428 'David Lloyd George' on 10th May 1996. The paper mill at Corpach opened in 1966 and sadly closed in 2005 with the loss of 126 jobs. Not only was this a bitter blow to the population of this isolated corner of Scotland, the loss of the rail flow is equally missed. The closure was blamed on the advent of the chip and pin system and the drastic reduction in the need for the type of paper formerly produced there. *(John Hooson)*

Opposite: 37428 'David Lloyd George' and 37410 'Aluminium 100' exit the Horseshoe Curve on 17th May 1996 with another loaded 7D19. This time the consist is aluminium ingots bound for Rogerstone in South Wales via Cardiff, plus paper again. The aluminium originates from the former British Aluminium Company smelter at Fort William, where the six feet of rainfall a year (on Ben Nevis!) ensures a plentiful supply of hydro-electricity. BAC merged with the Canadian company Alcan in 1982, and is known today as Alcan Primary Metals (Europe). The Fort William plant produces 40,000 tonnes each year cast into ten tonne ingots which are moved out by rail and road. The alumina is shipped to Blyth on the Northumberland coast for use at Lynemouth, with the Fort William requirement being sent from there by rail. *(John Hooson)*

Above: With Scotland and Wales enjoying regular Class 37 hauled passenger or sleeper trains right until 2006, it was common to find locos transferred regularly between the two countries. Back in the 1990s, as reported previously, most of the former Cardiff based machines ended up at Eastfield, Motherwell or Inverness working various Scottish duties. There was one exception, the elusive 37429 'Eisteddfod Genedlaethol' which essentially escaped regular duty north of the border. However, in 1991 a twist of fate saw it move to Thornaby depot which oddly enough then took responsibility for the former Motherwell based cement flows. The result was that 37429 made a few appearances on the Oxwellmains to Aberdeen cement flows before a further transfer to Crewe in 1992 and the Regional Railways passenger pool for the North West and North Wales. And here is the proof: 7th July 1992 at Niddrie Junction and 6A33 Oxwellmains to Aberdeen cement with 37429 and its Trainload Construction branding. *(Jim Ramsay/Nick Meskell collection)*

'OOR WULLIE'

Throughout railway history, depots and enthusiasts have selected specfic locomotives as mascots or pet engines. 37025 'Inverness TMD' is a well known Scottish favourite and the staff at Stratford TMD in east London are famous for their inspirational and enriching adoption of certain 37s. Perhaps 'Sister Dora', 37116 springs to mind or 37023 (over page) and prior to all this, there were the famous Class 47s with their silver roofs. In Scotland things were done on a lesser scale but nevertheless they were equally meaningful and welcome. The West Highland White Terrier (or Westie) was Eastfield's logo and it's still used today on certain locos while Inverness depot had the Highland Stag motif. The personalisation of Scottish locomotives faded out in the 1990s with one exception - 37275. From relative obscurity, the formerly Welsh machine was named 'Oor Wullie' at Springburn works on 14th October 1993. Formerly in the Civil Engineers 'Dutch' livery, a shiny coat of BR Blue was also applied and with reallocation to Inverness from September 1992 and then Motherwell in 1994, 37275 was a Scottish celebrity. Indecipherable and unpronounceable to just about everybody south of Carlisle, 'Oor Wullie' was an iconic young Scottish clod who first appeared lurking around the streets of Dundee in 1936 courtesy of the cartoon strip 'The Broons' in the Sunday Post newspaper. Today he has his own fan club!

Page 50: Looking neat and tidy, the indisputable 37275 hammers through Carnoustie with a lengthy rake of OTAs on 19th May 1995. The train is 6A15 from Mossend to Aberdeen. Note the nameplate is slightly higher on the bodysides than usual. 37402 was first with this name, revealed in a ceremony at Glasgow Queen Street on 14th December 1985. This loco carried the plates until 1993 before it was transferred to Crewe. A year later, 37402 was 'Bont-Y-Bermo'. Likewise, 37275 had a previous name. During its days working off Immingham, it was christened 'Stainless Pioneer' in December 1988. *(Jim Ramsay/Nick Meskell collection)*

Opposite top: A wet day at Oban on 18th June 1994 and a gleaming 'Oor Wullie' idles in the shadow of the Colosseum-like McCaig's Tower. 37275 put in a few appearances on the Oban line during this year. On both 9th and 11th July, it worked the previously mentioned 1Y03, 09.50 from Glasgow Queen Street, returning south with 1Y02 at 16.00. *(Nick Meskell collection)*

Opposite bottom: 37275 with 37201 double-head a loaded 6D52 Aberdeen to Mossend as they pass Buckingham Junction, the former site of Dundee TMD on 13th February 1995. 37201 carries the name 'Saint Margaret' which it received in a ceremony at Dunfermline station in November 1993. This loco was another ex-Welsh machine to make it north. Unlike many of the locomotives featured in this book, both 37201 and 37275 survived the cutter's torch and are preserved today. Withdrawn as early as September 1996, 37201 was stored at Bescot and then moved to Barrow Hill in August 2002. Privately owned today, the loco remains at Barrow Hill in a coat of 'Dutch' with the big 'T' Transrail branding. Minus nameplates the loco is described as under restoration. For 'Oor Wullie' the story was different. Surviving until January 1999, 37275 was bought for preservation in June 2004. On moving to the Wensleydale Railway, in a matter of days, the loco was repaired and started up! Owned by Bedale Railway Engines Limited (who also own 37175, 37198, 37414 and 37905), the loco was moved to the Weardale Railway in August 2006 and further restoration is ongoing. *(Jim Ramsay/Nick Meskell collection)*

THE 'BASHING' YEARS

Anbody with an interest in Class 37 haulage in the 1980s or 1990s would have surely headed to Scotland with a large rucksack and a 'Freedom of Scotland' 7 or 14 day ticket. If you were on the West Highland line in the 1980s, you would surely stumble on 'Loch Rannoch' 37012 or in later years 'Loch Long' 37407 and if you headed north from Inverness it was 37025 or 37418. The 1990s were very different. The services were unpredictable and instead of Oban, Mallaig and Wick, it was Aberdeen, Kyle and Perth. The blue livery was now yellow, grey, white and red and the temperature went from steam heat to electric heat to no heat! Here are the moves of a 37 basher from 5th August 1990 - a Sunday!

47701	00.10 Inverness to Perth
47595	06.12 Perth to Inverness
47644	10.10 Inverness to Forres
37262	11.08 Forres to Inverness
37261	12.36 Inverness to Aberdeen (with 37262 dead in tow)
37156	15.05 Aberdeen to Elgin
37708	16.32 Elgin to Dyce
37262	18.19 Dyce to Inverness
37262	20.45 Inverness to Aberdeen

Page 52: 37156 would appear to need some kind of help if the wording is correct on the headcode box! What it was for and what it meant is a mystery but there's no problem with this fine machine as it basks in the sunshine at Elgin on this fine sunny Sunday afternoon. Note the temporary headlight! By the mid-1980s all Inverness Type 3s (and indeed Class 26s too) had a headlight or spotlight of some kind. The idea was to help the driver spot cattle which had strayed onto the line or perhaps more importantly, it helped farmers (or pedestrians) at the many remote crossings to see an approaching train (could they not hear it?).

Opposite: Now you see me, now you don't or perhaps, 'he's behind you!....' 37262 at Inverness prior to departure with the 12.36 to Aberdeen... or at least that appeared to be the plan. 'Dounreay' had worked in with the 09.27 from Aberdeen and was ready here to depart with the 12.36 return when suddenly 37261 appeared and coupled up. As the story goes 'Caithness' had just come off repair and required a test run. The easiest option - probably for a Sunday anyway - was to have it pilot a service train and that is what happened. With 37262 available in case of failure this ensemble set off on time for the 108 mile journey to Aberdeen. Just under two and a half hours later and safely at Aberdeen, 37261 was uncoupled and stabled leaving 37262 to happily return with the 18.10 to Inverness. It really can't be underestimated what an incredibly hard life the seven Class 37s based at Inverness in the 1980s had, nor for that matter, what a sterling job Inverness TMD staff did to keep their tiny fleet as fit and operational as they did. In 1990, steam heat was a thing of the past and these trains were simply no heat. Pretty much since the dawn of diesels in Scotland, the Class 24s, 25s and 26s always had steam heat boilers - even in summer - as it may well have been sunny and bright in Inverness but at 06.00 at Kyle or Wick - even in mid-summer - could be cold and wet. 37261 survives today, working for DRS.

All photos and 'moves' by Peter Scott

Two years later and another week in Scotland produced yet more memorable events. By this time the ISSA and RAJV pools were in full swing and not a 37/4 could be found! The increase in modern DMUs was a sign of the times and the death knell for the loco hauled train.

Wednesday 22nd July 1992

87005	04.31 Carlisle to Glasgow
156445	06.33 Glasgow to Dunblane
37175+37170	07.39 Dunblane to Edinburgh
37175	11.30 Edinburgh to Inverness
37196	16.27 Inverness to Edinburgh
37196	21.22 Edinburgh to Perth

Thursday 23rd July 1992

156447+158703	01.20 Perth to Pitlochry
158702	02.13 Pitlochry to Perth
37196	07.08 Perth to Edinburgh
37196	11.30 Edinburgh to Inverness
37088	18.36 Inverness to Kyle

Page 54 top: There is something exceptionally pleasing about 37088. Whether it be the small white fleet number, the unusual 088 in black numerals on the right hand nose door, the all over grey livery, the black headcode boxes or perhaps the name 'Clydesdale', this is a monster of monsters, make no mistake of that. Away from its better known days at Inverness, 37088 was just another Eastern Region loco which was stored out of service between 1978 and 1980. In the photo, the loco prepares to depart for the 82.25 mile journey. At Kyle, both loco and stock stabled and returned to Inverness with the 06.50 on the Friday morning. *(Peter Scott)*

Page 54 inset: It would appear the 07.08 commuter train from Perth to Edinburgh (via Falkirk and Linlithgow) was 'the train' for 37 bashers in 1992. With 37175+37170 approaching Dunblane in the photo, this particular journey and the full diagram is described earlier in the book as 'demanding' and it certainly was. If the loco stuck to diagram it ended up back at Perth the same evening, only to work the same trains the following day. *(Peter Scott)*

Opposite: Moving nicely towards the next feature and the 24th July 1999 with 37023 'Stratford' at Tulloch having failed on a railtour. Don't be fooled by the Westie logo, 37023 was a true Eastern Region machine, despite spending a couple of years in Scotland between 1987 and 1989. With the spread of the 'Red Death' in Scotland, the days of the Class 37/0s were numbered, which prompted Mercia Charters to run a railtour to Fort William and Oban. Starting at Northampton, haulage came in the shape of 37013+37165 on an overnight train across the border. At Mossend 37023+37114 took over and worked to Fort William. On the return, 37023 suffered traction motor problems and was duly dumped at Tulloch. This left the former Inverness based 37114 to work the **12** coach train solo to Crianlarich where it ran round and performed heroics to Oban and back (seen opposite at Oban). Help came on the return when 37116 was coupled to 37114 and the pair worked right through to Rugby. *(Peter Scott/Nick Meskell collection)*
(All 'moves' by Peter Scott)
(The 'Red Death' was not a plague, it was the introduction of the Class 66s)

Opposite: Over the last 25 years, there have been a staggering number of railtours in Scotland worked by Class 37s, whether enthusiast tours which specify a Class 37 or days out by rail which just use whatever loco is available. A book of this nature could never record all these trains so here is one example, Pathfinder Tours' 'The Skirl Revisited'. This mammoth was a sequel to the famous 'Skirl o' the Pipes' tours from the 1980s and used pretty much what was the best of the so called 'heritage' traction available. In the photo opposite, 37196 brings a rake of Inter City Mk1s to the Highlands, crossing the magnificent Glenfinnan Viaduct on a journey from Fort William to Mallaig on 12th June 1993. Having featured previously in this book in Railfreight Red Stripe, the loco was in 'Dutch' by this time. 37196 worked the train solo from Fort William to Mallaig and back. Previously it had arrived in multiple with 37156 from Mossend and it departed from Fort William with 37410 - see full loco list below. All in all, featuring five different 37s, this was certainly a great tour but 26003 from Crewe to Mossend was pretty outrageous and on the return, a Class 58 coming on at Tebay loop must also score top marks! In total 16 different locos were used. *(Nick Meskell collection)*

The Skirl Revisited - 11th/12 June 1993

D7018	Minehead to Bishops Lydeard
47674	Bishops Lydeard to Birmingham NS
31106+31537	Birmingham NS to Crewe
26003+31144	Crewe to Carlisle
26003+26005	Carlisle to Mossend
37156+37196	Mossend to Fort William
37196	Fort William to Mallaig
37196	Mallaig to Fort William
37196+37410	Fort William to Glasgow Central
56074	Glasgow Central to Ayr
56128	Ayr to Stranraer
56123	Stranraer to Ayr
37106+37692	Ayr to Tebay loop
58018	Tebay loop to Bristol TM

Above: Loco change at Ayr with 37106+37692 taking over from 56123. This is probably quite a rare opportunity to see a 'Dutch' liveried loco so clean! *(Nick Meskell collection)*

Scottish Class 37 DVDs

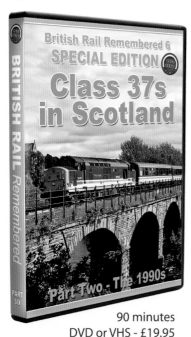

90 minutes
DVD or VHS - £19.95

Class 37s in Scotland – Part Two - The 1990s

To accompany our third Scottish Class 37 book, this special DVD features film from the 1990s. Split into four categories, Passenger trains, Sleepers, Luxury trains and Freight, this programme looks at the complete Class 37 scene from this decade.

'Passenger Trains' features many no-heat locos including 37099, 37100, 37152, 37175, 37294, 36510 and many of the ex-Welsh 37/4s transferred to Scotland including 37427, 37428, 37430 and 37431 working Inverness – Edinburgh services.

'Sleepers' looks at the Inverness and Fort William trains with pairs of 37/0s and 37/5s climbing Slochd summit. It wasn't always matching pairs in Inter City livery with 37697+37696 in coal branding and 37/0s 37170 and 37255. The Fort William sleeper features a mixed bag of 37/4s like 37403 in BR Green, 37406, 37410, 37423, 37424, 37425 and 37430.

'Luxury trains' features Inter City Land Cruises, the Royal Scotsman and other Pullmans and Railtours. Locos include 37152+37221 shunting at Kyle and 37099 and BR Blue 37275 'Oor Wullie' working the Royal Scotsman.

The **'Freight'** section covers loaded and empty OTAs on the Highland Mainline and various double-headed trains on the West Highland line including EPS 37, 37606! Plus, pairs of 37s on MGRs and tankers on the G&SW route.

All in all this is a tremendous recollection of what was an interesting decade for the Class 37 in Scotland. From the final days of Large Logo to the EWS years, the 1990s had it all.

52 pages - Full colour - £9.95

60 pages - Full colour - £9.95

60 pages - Full colour - £9.95

Class 37s in the 1980s and 1994
80 mins - DVD or VHS - £14.95

This DVD includes a 20 minute feature on Class 26s and 27s in the 1980s
105 mins - DVD or VHS - £19.95

This DVD includes a look at 37s in Scotland today with 37029 working the Royal Scotsman
115 mins - DVD or VHS - £17.95

Please contact us for full details of all of these items and a copy of our free catalogue.

Post: Train Crazy, FREEPOST, Blackpool. FY4 1BR.
Telephone & Fax: 01253 346005
email: admin@train-crazy.co.uk
website: www.train-crazy.co.uk

For full details of all these titles, please contact us or visit our website:

www.train-crazy.co.uk

Many other titles available.